GRADE 2 GRAMMAR 1

Fun-filled Activities

The Sentence

A sentence is a group of words that is complete in itself. A sentence starts with a capital letter and ends with an end mark.

The dog is sleeping.	A beautiful bird
A sentence	**not a sentence**

QUICK CHECK

An end mark can be a period (.), question mark (?) or an exclamatory mark (!)

Read the groups of words given below. Write S if it is a sentence and N if it is not a sentence.

1. We went to the park. ☐
2. On the swings ☐
3. The boys went on swings for an hour. ☐
4. The bird and nest ☐
5. The girls are skipping. ☐
6. In the winter ☐
7. The cat watched the bird on the tree. ☐
8. All of us had fun at the park. ☐

Try it!

Write a sentence about yourself.

____

Parts of a Sentence

A sentence has two parts – naming part and telling part.

Naming part of a sentence

Bobby rode on the merry-go-round.

naming part

The merry-go-round is high.

naming part

A naming part tells us who or what the sentence is about.

Bobby is the naming part.

The merry-go-round tells what this sentence is about.

QUICK CHECK

The naming part can be a **person, place, animal**, or **thing.**

Circle the naming part of these sentences.

1. Father and Carl went to the pool.
2. The day was hot.
3. The water was cold to touch.
4. Carl jumped into the pool with his father.
5. He took a tube to swim.
6. Carl liked to be in the cool water.
7. Father had fun in swimming too.

Try it!

Write a naming part for this sentence.

__________________________________ went for a ride.

Parts of a Sentence

Telling part of a sentence.

Bobby rode on the merry-go-round.
telling part

The merry-go-round is high.
telling part

QUICK CHECK
The telling part of the sentence has a word that shows an action or what, how or where someone or something is.

A telling part tells us what someone or something does. It also tells us what/how someone or something is.

rode on the merry-go-round tells what Bobby did.

is high tells where the merry-go-round is.

Underline the telling part of these sentences.

1. Mary and Joy help mom in the kitchen.
2. Mother makes rice and fish for supper.
3. Joy wipes the plates.
4. Mary lays the table for supper.
5. Mother, Mary and Joy are happy.
6. They like to work together.

Try it!
Write a telling part for this sentence.
Kate and Jim ______________________________

Put the Words in Order!

Which of these sentences uses the correct order of words? Tick the right answer.

1. I like eat to oranges.
2. Kim went to bed at 9.
3. Linda plays dolls with her.
4. Sail boat across the river.

Can you put the words in the correct order to form meaningful sentences? Write down the sentences in the correct word order.

1. Lia a dog pet has

 ____

2. dog her pug is a named Tuff

 ____

3. one year old is Tuff only

 ____

4. has it brown a coat soft

 ____

5. fond of eating it bread and milk is

 ____

6. made a kennel Lia has Tuff for

 ____

7. takes walk Lia her dog for evening in the a

 ____

8. care takes Lia of Tuff good

 ____

QUICK CHECK

Don't forget to begin the sentence with a capital letter and end with an end mark.

Try it! Use the word 'kennel' to make a sentence.

____

Statements

A statement is a sentence that tells us something. A statement begins with a capital letter and ends with a period (.)

Neo likes to fly kites.

The kite is red and blue.

These sentences have capital letters and full stop placed incorrectly. Can you rewrite these statements correctly?

1. many people like to Fly. kites

   ____

2. kites Are made of. Paper

   ____

3. a kite is shaped. like a Diamond

   ____

4. nick likes to fly kites Too.

   ____

5. he has Made a kite. Shaped like a bird

   ____

6. it is. Fun to fly kites

   ____

Try it!

What kind of a kite would you like to fly? Write a statement about it.

____

____

Questions

A question is a sentence that asks for some information. A question begins with a capital letter and ends with a question mark (?)

Where are my books?

Have you seen my bag?

QUICK CHECK

Questions often begin with **who, what, when, where, why, how, do, did, will, can, is, am, are, was and were,** and so on.

Three of these sentences have full stops (.) in place of question mark (?). Identify and rewrite them using a question mark.

1. Mary and her family went to the zoo.

   ____

2. How far is the zoo.

   ____

3. They reached there in two hours.

   ____

4. Which animals did Mary see in the zoo.

   ____

5. Did they see the white tiger.

   ____

6. They had fun at the zoo.

   ____

Try it!

Write a question that you would ask Mary about her visit to the zoo.

____

Statements and Questions

Statement

- I like to play football.
- The bird is on the tree.

Question

- Which is your favourite game?
- Where is the bird?

QUICK CHECK

A question is used to ask something.
A statement tells us something.

Read each sentence below. Write 'St' for statement and 'Q' for question.

1. It is Tim's birthday today. ☐
2. How old is Tim? ☐
3. All his friends have come to wish him. ☐
4. The children are dressed in nice clothes. ☐
5. At what time will the party begin? ☐
6. I can see the beautifully decorated cake with pink and white icing. ☐
7. When will Tim cut the cake? ☐
8. There are many chairs in a row. ☐
9. Will the children play Musical Chairs? ☐
10. It will be fun at the party. ☐

Try it!

Put a full stop (.) at the end of the statement and a question mark (?) at the end of the question.

1. Where is James going with his sister
2. I am going to the beach

Exclamations

An exclamatory sentence expresses feelings. It shows excitement or surprise. Such sentences begin with a capital letter and end with an exclamation mark (!).

The garden is so beautiful!

Such pretty flowers it has!

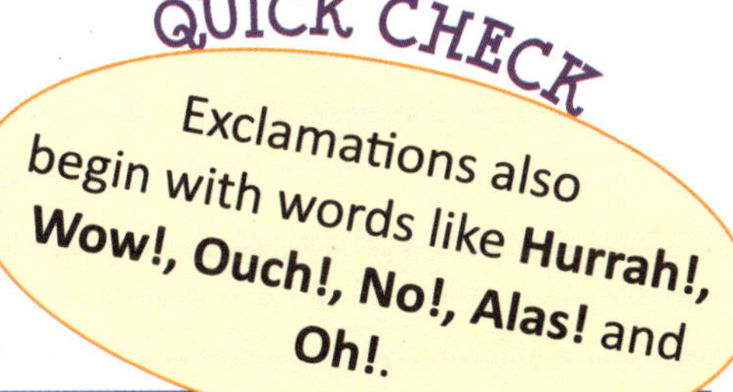

Can you identify exclamations from the statements below? Put exclamation marks (!) for exclamatory sentences and full stops (.) for statements.

1. Jim and Tim went to the Shoe House
   ______
2. The Shoe House was so big
   ______
3. The boys ran inside the house
   ______
4. Oh, it was beautiful
   ______
5. Jim and Tim were happy
   ______
6. They played in the Shoe House
   ______
7. It was awesome
   ______

Try it!

Your mother bought a toy for you. Write an exclamatory sentence to express your answer.

____

Commands

A command is a sentence that tells you to do something. A command begins with a capital letter. It ends with a period (.).

Don't shut the door.

Open the windows.

QUICK CHECK

Statements usually begin with a noun or pronoun. Commands usually begin with a verb.

Tia is making fruit cream. Grandfather is telling Tia what to do.

Rearrange the words and write each command correctly.

1. apples and strawberries, cherries pomegranate pick up

   ____

2. all the wash fruits.

   ____

3. and remove cut cherries into half its pit.

   ____

4. pomegranate peel the.

   ____

5. and apples into chop strawberries small pieces.

   ____

6. sugar in put cream and a bowl and mix it.

   ____

7. all and mix the now add fruits well.

   ____

Try it!

Think of one command your mother gave you. Write it down.

____

Putting it Together!

Complete the sentences using words from the box. Then, write 'St' for statements, 'Q' for questions, 'E' for exclamations and 'C' for commands.

in the bushes	there	ball	puppy in his hands
move	the garden	the mud	ball in his hand

1. Amy looked around ______________ [ ]
2. Was someone hiding ______________ [ ]
3. Amy had a ______________ [ ]
4. Oh, he dropped the ______________ [ ]
5. He bent to ______________ [ ]
6. There were footprints on ______________ [ ]
7. Who was ______________ [ ]
8. Don't ______________ [ ]
9. Oh, it was a ______________ [ ]
10. Amy lifted the ______________ [ ]

QUICK CHECK

Don't forget to use:

- Period (.) at the end of a statement and command.
- Question mark (?) at the end of a question.
- Exclamation mark (!) at the end of an exclamatory sentence.

Naming Words or Nouns

A noun is a word that names a person, place, animal or thing.

Pam goes to the park.

The word 'Pam' names a person.

The word 'park' names a place.

Pam has a puppy.

The word 'puppy' names an animal.

Take the puppy on the bicycle.

The word 'bicycle' names a thing.

Here is a list of words. Select and separate these words into the different categories of nouns as given in the table.

book	lion	Jim	doctor	dog	hen	Kate	school
pen	comb	house	pool	fish	Sim	egg	chair

Person	Place	Animal	Thing

Try it!

Write the names of a person, place, animal and thing that begin with the letter "R".

____

To the Camp!

Pat went camping. Read the text below and circle the nouns.

Pat and Neo went on a camping trip. The boys packed their bags. They packed shirts, shorts, socks and shoes. Neo took his hat. Pat took his books and toys. They went to the hills. The Sun was shining, the birds were singing, and the bees were buzzing. There were sheep too. Many boys and girls were on the camp. Both the boys went on a boat. It was fun at the camp.

Try it!

Write name of one person, place, animal and thing that you saw on your way to school yesterday.

____

____

____

One and More than One

Nouns can name one or more than one.

A monkey is jumping on the tree.

The noun **monkey** names one.

The birds flew away from the tree.

The noun **birds** names more than one.

Many nouns that name more than one usually end with **s**.

Write the correct noun and complete the sentence.

1. A __________ and two birds were good friends. (tortoise/tortoises)
2. They lived on the banks of a __________ in a forest. (river/rivers)
3. The birds went to many __________. (place/places)
4. The tortoise felt sad that he could not go with them. He did not have __________. (wing/wings)
5. He told the birds to hold each end of a long __________ with their __________. (stick/sticks, beak/beaks)
6. He will hold the middle part of the stick with his __________. (mouth/mouths)
7. So he can fly with the __________ too! (bird/birds)

Try it!

Write names of parts of your body that are more than one.

____

Nouns Ending with -es

Many nouns that end with **s, sh, ch** and **x** add **-es** to name more than one.

bench- benches   box- boxes

dish- dishes   glass- glasses

Fill in the word grid by making these nouns more than one.

fox   dress   brush   bus   peach   watch   bush   sandwich

	b			h										
											f			
					w									b
			p	e		c								r
					t									
								d	r					
		b												
					s				w					s

Try it!

Correct the sentence.

The boxs are in the coachs.

____

Nouns Ending with -ies

Some nouns end with **y** and have a consonant before it. Such nouns name more than one by removing **y** and adding **–ies**.

puppy- puppies

lady- ladies

Some nouns end in **y** and have a vowel before it. Such nouns name more than one just by adding **s**.

boy- boys

key- keys

Write the word that names more than one for each noun below.

1. monkey - ______________
2. toy - ______________
3. baby - ______________
4. cherry - ______________
5. story - ______________
6. day - ______________
7. berry - ______________
8. tray - ______________
9. city - ______________
10. way - ______________

a, e, i, o, u are vowels.
b, c, d, f, g, h, j, k, l, m, n, p, q, r, s, t, v, w, x, y, z are consonants.
For nouns that end with **y**, check whether **y** has a vowel or a consonant before it... to name it as more than one

Try it!

How will you write the word fairy to name more than one?

____

Nouns Ending with -ves

Some nouns end with **f** or **fe**. Such nouns name more than one by removing **f** or **fe** and adding –**ves**.

loaf- loaves

knife- knives

Circle the correct word that names more than one of the words given below.

1.	calf	–	calfs	calves
2.	elf	–	elves	elfs
3.	half	–	halfs	halves
4.	chef	–	chefs	cheves
5.	wolf	–	wolves	wolfs
6.	life	–	lifes	lives
7.	giraffe	–	giraves	giraffes
8.	leaf	–	leaves	leafs
9.	cliff	–	cliffs	clives
10.	self	–	selves	selfs
11.	shelf	–	shelfs	shelves
12.	roof	–	roves	roofs
13.	thief	–	thiefs	thieves
14.	wife	–	wives	wifes
15.	chief	–	chiefs	chieves

QUICK CHECK

Not all words ending in f or fe add - ves to them after removing f or fe. Some words just add –s to the words that end in f or fe

Chefs, giraffes, roofs, chiefs, cliffs

Try it!

How will you write the word 'scarf' to show more than one?

____

Nouns Written Differently

Some nouns are written differently to denote more than one.

man – men

ox – oxen

child – children

foot – feet

Some nouns do not change to denote more than one.

one fish – many fish

one sheep – three sheep

Change these words to name more than one.

1. woman – women
2. mouse – ____________
3. fish – ____________
4. goose – ____________
5. child – ____________
6. ox – ____________
7. sheep – ____________
8. deer – ____________
9. dice – ____________
10. tooth – ____________

Try it!

Can you name the picture? What would you write for more than one of it?

____________________ ____________________

A or An

'A' and 'An' are articles. We use 'a' or 'an' before nouns that denote one.

'A' is used with noun words that begin with a consonant.

A bird sat on a rock.

'An' is used with noun words that begin with a vowel or vowel sound.

An emu laid an egg

Tick a or an for these words.

1. (a/an) apple and (a/an) pineapple
2. (a/an) monkey and (a/an) elephant
3. (a/an) banana and (a/an) orange
4. (a/an) ostrich and (a/an) owl

QUICK CHECK

Before writing a/an check if the word begins with a consonant or vowel/vowel sound. Do you remember the vowels and consonants?

Write a or an in the blanks and complete the text.

1. One day I saw ________ cat.
2. The cat was sitting on ________ fence under ________ umbrella.
3. The cat was having ________ ice cream.
4. ________ mouse came running near the cat.
5. It had ________ box.
6. There was ______ pen, ______ fork, ______ ink pot, ______ watch and ______ bat in the bag.
7. The mouse ran into ______ hole.

Try it!

Write names of 3 things you have in your school bag using a or an.

____

Some Special Nouns

Special names of people, animals and places are called proper nouns. We begin all proper nouns with a capital letter.

Sim is my friend.

He has a pet cat. His cat's name is Kitty.

Sim and Kitty are proper nouns.

Underline the proper nouns in the paragraph given below. Are they written correctly? Mark each letter that should be in capital and rewrite the letter.

J

james is popo's friend. He went to meet his friend, popo yesterday.

≡

He took his pet squirrel jojo with him. There he met uncle tim and aunt mary. popo has a pet duck. He calls it doyo. popo gave jojo a few nuts to eat. jojo enjoyed eating them. Soon joy, kate, neo and linda came there. They all made a duck house for doyo.

Try it!

Imagine you have a pet. What name would you like to give it? Now, write a sentence about your imaginary pet.

____

Special Names of Places

Proper nouns are also special names of places.

I live in London.

London is the special name of a city.

Noun	Special names/Proper nouns
street	Oak Lane
school	Montfort School
apartments	Royal Apartments
park	Yellow Stone Park
city	New York
state	Texas
country	France

Ronny wants to meet his friend. Draw lines to help him find his way to Royal Apartments from the park. Pick words from the box and write names of the places that fall on his way.

QUICK CHECK

Names of clubs, museums, hotels, malls and restaurants are also proper nouns.

Palm Street, Lane Street, Regent Park, Royal Apartments, Mont Fort School, Club 65,

Try it!

Do you know your address? Write it here with the name of your country.

____

____

What day is it?

Proper nouns are also used to denote days, months and days like festivals and holidays.

Christmas is celebrated on 25th December every year.

This year Christmas falls on Sunday.

Birthday Time!

Write names of any of your 5 friends with their birthdays. Also write which day it is on their birthday.

Try it! List out three holidays or special days you will celebrate this year.

Terrific Titles!

Proper nouns also name titles of books, movies, television shows, plays and songs.

Have you read the book Smith and Harry?

I like to watch the cartoon Tin-Tin.

QUICK CHECK

Words like and, the, a, of, when written between titles should not be written with capital letter. The first word of the title however begins with a capital letter.

Rewrite the following sentences, put the underlined titles in capital letters.

1. Our family went to watch the toy story.

____

2. Teacher read the story the chocolate factory to us.

____

3. Sam likes to watch pokemon.

____

4. We are going to act the little mermaid.

____

Fill this about your mother. Don't forget to use capital letters where needed.

Name ____

Her birthday ____

Street Address ____

City ____

Title of favourite book ____

Title of favourite TV show ____

Best Friend ____

Favourite place to visit ____

Action Words or Verbs

A verb is a word that denotes actions. It tells us what people, things, animals or creatures do.

Verbs also tell us what is happening.

I jump. I shake.

I dance. I hop.

I will move and not stop.

The words jump, shake, dance and hop show actions. They are verbs.

Circle the verb in each sentence.

1. Jane helps dad in the garden.
2. Dad mows the lawn.
3. Jane pulls the weeds.
4. Dad picks vegetables.
5. Then they paint the fence.
6. Dad gives her ice cream as a treat after dinner.

Use verbs from the box to complete the poem.

The Sun shines. The birds ________.

The wind ________. The river ________.

Rabbits ________. Girls ________.

And We ________!

flows	chirp	blows	shines
sing	stop	hop	

Try it! Write two sentences on how you help your Dad. Underline the verbs.

____

____

Is, Am, Are

The verbs, is, am and are tell us what things are like. They denote the time 'now'.

I am a girl.

My dress is clean.

My shoes are black.

QUICK CHECK

Words that use is, am, are
I: am
He, she, it, this, that (one noun)- :is
We, they, these, those, more than one noun: are

Use is, am or are to fill in the blanks.

1. Robin ________ a baker.
2. Paul and John ________ his friends.
3. They ________ at Robin's bakery.
4. It ________ a cold morning today.
5. It ________ 8 o'clock. The men ________ hungry now.
6. Robin says, "I ________ hungry too."
7. The cookies ________ ready.
8. "We ________ happy now," say Paul and John.

Try it!

Write three sentences about yourself using is, am, are.

____

____

____

Was, Were

The verbs, was and were tell us what things were like in the past.

Peter was sad yesterday.

His toys were broken.

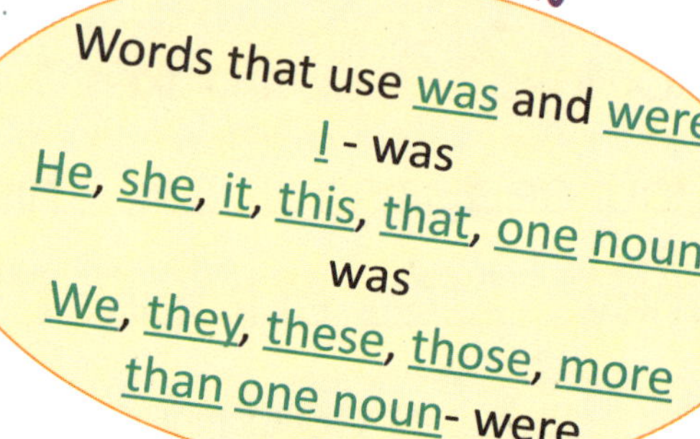

Use was or were to fill in the blanks.

1. It ________ music class on Monday.
2. Some children ________ late for the class.
3. Kim and Jacob ________ the first to come.
4. Pinto ________ the last to come.
5. We ________ in our seats soon.
6. Drums ________ in the class. We played them.
7. The teacher ________ pleased with us.
8. The boys and girls ________ happy.

Try it!

Write a sentence with the word 'flute' using was or were.

____

____

____

Has, Have, Had

The verbs, has, have and had tell us that something belongs to someone.

Has and have are used in the present.

Peter has three books.

The girls have a pencil in their hand.

Had is used in the past.

Last year, Lucy had a toy car.

QUICK CHECK

Words that use has, have and had ! - have
He, she, it, this, that, one noun- has
We, they, these, those, more than one noun- have
Had is used with all the nouns and naming parts of a sentence

Use has or have to fill in the blanks.

1. Dane ________ two pet cats.
2. The cats ________ small ears.
3. One cat ________ white fur.
4. The other cat ________ brown fur.
5. Both cats ________ thin tails.
6. The brown cat ________ blue eyes.
7. The white cat ________ stripes.

Rewrite these sentences using had.

1. Jenny has a party yesterday. ________________________
2. She has a crown on her head. ________________________
3. Her friends have flowers on their hair. ________________________

Try it!

Write two sentences about what you have in your school bag.

____

____

Pronouns

A pronoun is a word used in place of a noun. A pronoun must match the noun it replaces.

I, you, he, she and it are singular pronouns.

Sentences with nouns	**Pronouns in place of nouns**
Daniel has a football.	He has a football.
The football is big.	It is big.
Daniel's sister also plays with it.	She also plays with it.

QUICK CHECK

The pronoun I is always written in capitals.
It is used for animals and things without life.

Pick and circle the correct pronoun to replace the underlined noun in each sentence.

1. Jason went on a trip to the Safari.	He	It
2. The Safari was hot and dry.	They	It
3. Jason's uncle saw a Prickly Pear.	He	It
4. The prickly pear does not have leaves.	We	It
5. Jason saw a Red Tegu!	She	He
6. A Red Tegu is a lizard found in Africa.	It	They
7. Jason was scared!	He	She
8. Jason's mother and father were a little scared, too.	They	We

Try it!

Write two sentences about an animal you are scared of. Use three pronouns in it.

____

____

Plural Pronouns

Pronouns we, you and they are plural pronouns. They are used in place of plural nouns.

Sharks are water animals. They are water animals.

Ronny and I saw a shark. We saw a shark.

Rewrite the sentences using pronouns in place of the underlined nouns.

1. Jags and Nora are going to the sea shore.

____

2. Did Jags and Nora see the shark?

____

QUICK CHECK

The pronoun you is used for both singular and plural nouns.

3. Sharks don't eat people, so Jags and I are not in danger.

____

4. Mom and Jags want to see snails. Snails are so cute!

____

5. "Have Jags and Nora ever seen a snail?" asked Mom.

____

6. Jags and Dad also saw a crab.

____

7. Crabs always walk sideways.

____

8. "Nora and I are having so much fun on the shore," said Jags to mom.

____

Try it!

What would you and your brother like to do at the sea shore? Write it using 'We'.

____

____

I, We, Me and Us

We use I and we in the naming part of a sentence.

I like to dance.

We will wear frocks in the dance show.

We use me and us in the telling part of a sentence.

My mother is calling me.

The tailor will stitch the dress for us.

Rewrite the sentences using correct pronouns in place of underlined ones.

QUICK CHECK
Name yourself last when talking about yourself and another person.

1. Mom and me went to see a magic show.

____

2. The usher gave I a ticket and showed we where to sit.

____

3. i could see the rabbits coming out of the hat.

____

4. us also saw paper flowers changing to roses.

____

5. Us had great time!

____

6. me hope Mom takes I to another show soon!

____

Try it!

Write about a gift you got on your birthday. Write a sentence using I and me.

____

____

Answer Key

Page 2

1. S
2. N
3. S
4. N
5. S
6. N
7. S
8. S

Page 3

Naming parts

1. Father and Carl
2. The day
3. The water
4. Carl
5. He
6. Carl
7. Father

Page 4

Telling part

1. help mom in the kitchen
2. makes rice and fish for supper
3. wipes the plates
4. lays the table for supper
5. are happy
6. like to work together

Page 5

Only sentence 2 is in correct order

1. Lia has a pet dog.
2. Her dog is a pug named Tuff.
3. Tuff is only one year old.
4. It has a soft brown coat.
5. It is fond of eating bread and milk.
6. Lia has made a kennel for Tuff.
7. Lia takes her dog for a walk in the evening.
8. Lia takes good care of Tuff.

Page 6

1. Many people like to fly kites.
2. Kites are made of paper.
3. A kite is shaped like a diamond.
4. Nick likes to fly kites too.
5. He has made a kite shaped like a bird.
6. It is fun to fly kites.

Page 7

1. Mary and her family went to the zoo.
2. How far is the zoo?
3. They reached there in two hours.
4. Which animals did Mary see in the zoo?
5. Did they see the white tiger?
6. They had fun at the zoo

Page 8

1. St
2. Q
3. St
4. St
5. Q
6. St
7. Q
8. St
9. Q
10. St

Page 9

1. Jim and Tim went to the Shoe House.
2. The Shoe House was so big!
3. The boys ran inside the house.
4. Oh, it was beautiful!
5. Jim and Tim were happy.
6. They played in the Shoe House.
7. It was awesome!

Page 10

1. Pick up apples, strawberries, cherries and pomegranate
2. Wash all the fruits.
3. Cut cherries into half and remove its pit.
4. Peel the pomegranate.
5. Chop apples and strawberries into small pieces.
6. Put sugar and cream in a bowl and mix it.
7. Now add all the fruits and mix well.

Page 11

1. Amy looked around the garden. St
2. Was someone hiding in the bushes? Q
3. Amy had a ball in his hands. St
4. Oh, he dropped the ball! E
5. He bent to pick up the ball. St
6. There were footprints on the mud. St
7. Who was there? Q
8. Don't move. C
9. Oh, it was a puppy! E
10. Amy lifted the puppy in his hands St

Page 12

Person	Place	Animal	Thing
Jim	house	lion	book
doctor	pool	dog	pen
Kate	school	fish	comb
Sim	hen	egg	chair

Page 13

Nouns

Pat, Neo, camp, boys, bag, shirts, shorts, socks, shoes, hat, books, toys, hills, sun, birds, bees, sheep, girls, boat

Page 14

1. tortoise
2. river
3. places
4. wings
5. stick, beaks
6. mouth
7. birds

Page 15

	b	u	s	h	e	s								
											f			
					w						o			b
			p	e	a	c	h	e	s		x			r
					t						e			u
					c			d	r	e	s	s	e	s
					h									h
		b	u	s	e	s								e
					s	a	n	d	w	i	c	h	e	s

Answer Key

Page 16

1. monkeys 2. toys 3. babies
4. cherries 5.stories 6. berries
7. days 8. trays 9. cities 10. ways

Page 17

1. calves 2. elves 3. halves 4. chefs
5. wolves 6. lives 7. giraffes 8. leaves
9. cliffs 10. selves 11. shelves 12. roofs
13. thieves 14. wives 15. schiefs

Page18

woman – women
mouse – mice
fish – fish
goose – geese
child – children
ox – oxen
sheep – sheep
deer – deer
dice – dice
tooth – teeth

Page 19

1. (an) apple and (a) pineapple
2. (a) monkey and (an) elephant
3. (a) banana and (an) orange
4. (an) ostrich and (an) owl

1. a 2. a, an 3. an 4. a
5. a 6. a, a, an, a, a 7. As

Page 20

Begin these words with capital

Jojo, Tim, Mary, Popo, Doyo, Joy, Kate, Neo, Linda

Page 21

Children will do on their own.

Page 22

Children have to attempt on their own. Answers will vary.

Page 23

1. Toy Story
2. The Chocolate Factory
3. Pokemon
4. The Little Mermaid

Children have to fill information about their mother. Answers will vary.

Page 24

Verbs:

1. helps 2.mows 3.pulls
4. picks 5.paint 6.gives

The birds chirp.
The wind blows.
The river flows.
Rabbits hop.
Girls sing.
And we stop!

Page 25

1. is 2. are 3. are 4. is
5. is, are 6. am 7. are 8. Are

Page 26

1. was 2. were 3. were 4. was
5. were 6. were 7. was 8. were

Page 27

1. has 2. have 3. has 4. has
5. have 6. has 7. has 8. has

1. Jenny had a party yesterday.
2. She had a crown on her head.
3. Her friends had flowers on their hair.

Page 28

1. She 2. It 3. He 4. It
5. He 6. It 7. He 8. They

Page 29

1. They are going to the sea shore.
2. Did they see the shark?
3. Sharks don't eat people, so we are not in danger.
4. Mom and Jags want to see snails. They are so cute!
5. "Have you ever seen a snail?" asked Mom.
6. They also saw a crab.
7. They always walk sideways.
8. "We are having so much fun on the shore," said Jags to mom.

Page 30

1. Mom and I went to see a magic show.
2. The usher gave me a ticket and showed us where to sit.
3. I could see the rabbits coming out of the hat.
4. We also saw paper flowers changing to roses.
5. We had great time!
6. I hope Mom takes me to another show soon!